RECONNECTING MEMORIES

Dreams No Longer Deferred

New & Selected Poems by Mwatabu S. Okantah

Africa World Press, Inc.

P.O. Box 1892
Trenton, NJ 08607

P.O. Box 48
Asmara, ERITREA

Africa World Press, Inc.

P.O. Box 1892
Trenton, NJ 08607

P.O. Box 48
Asmara, ERITREA

Book and Cover Design: Roger Dormann

Library of Congress Cataloging-in-Publication Data

Okantah, Mwatabu.
  Reconnecting memories : dreams no longer deferred : new & selected poems / by Mwatabu S. Okantah.
    p. cm.
  ISBN 1-59221-059-7 -- ISBN 1-59221-060-0 (pbk.)
  1. African Americans--Poetry. 2. Africa--Poetry. I. Title.

PS3565.K34R43 2003
811'.54—dc22

2003022896

in loving memory of my father

Wilbur Thomas Smith, Sr.
(October 16, 1921 to January 19, 2000)

Table of Contents

DEDICATION

To Aminah with profound love and gratitude because you inspired me to reclaim my life. You gave me another chance when I needed it most. You rescued me from my ugly Self. You believed in me when I was shaken in my belief in myself. You became my soul-mate when all I hoped for was a wife.

To all of my children: Janeia, Ta-Seti, Jamila, Afrikiti, Ile-Ife, Sowande and Berhane because you each chose me to be the father I always dreamed I could be.

And, a shout out to the following people for their steadfast encouragement, support, and their love:

Gladys Smith, Diana & Bill Smith, Kwame Nyamekye, Wangui wa Goro, Diedre Badejo, Chief Fela Sowande, Curtis Wilson, Halim el Dabh, Naomi Long Madgett, Al Henry, Murphy Ajayi, Gladys Bozeman, Carolyn Dukes, Chris McVay, Jackie Rowser, Eric Gould, Glenn Holmes, Bill Ransom, Kwaw David Whitaker, Torman Jahi, James G. Spady, Anthony "Da Boogieman" Rucker, Kelly Harris, Daniel Gray-Kontar, Cavani String Quartet, Moulaye Jobe, Kofoworola Ladipo, my PAS students and all those unnamed who are too numerous to mention.

ACKNOWLEDGEMENTS

"the black experience," "African morning" & "market day," *Beyond the Frontier: African-American Poetry for the 21st Century*, Ed. by E. Ethelbert Miller, c2002

"African tree" & "see her," *Journey to TimBookTu: An African-American Poetic Odyssey*, Ed. by Memphis Vaughan, Jr., c2002

"homeboy," *Blue Fifth Review*, Ed. by Sam Rasnake, Summer 2002

"red, white and bruised" & "slave times," TimBookTu.com, Ed. by Memphis Vaughan, Jr., April 4, 2002

"red, white and bruised," *Underground Poets Society*, Ed. by Antwian Crawford, November 2001

"a new sun rising," TimBookTu.com, Ed. by Memphis Vaughan, Jr., November 5, 2001

"poem for Africa," TimBookTu.com, Ed. by Memphis Vaughan, Jr., September 5, 2001

"to a black woman" & "a poet's poem," TimBookTu.com, Ed. by Memphis Vaughan, Jr., November 6, 2000

"African tree," TimBookTu.com, Ed. by Memphis Vaughan, Jr. October 2, 2000

"breakfast at the Ibis" & "warrior queen," TimBookTu.com, Ed. by Memphis Vaughan, Jr., September 5, 2000

"see her" & "Zoo Atlanta," TimBookTu.com, Ed. by Memphis Vaughan, Jr., July 5, 2000

"African morning" & "market day," TimBookTu.com, Ed. by Memphis Vaughan, Jr., June 5, 2000

"can we talk about race?" TimBookTu.com, Ed. by Memphis Vaughan, Jr., May 5, 2000

"see her," *Seeds: Wild Women, Wild Times,* Ed. by Efua Korantema,
Vol. 6, Winter 2000

"the black experience," *Warpland: Black Writers Approaching The
Millenium,* Ed. by B. J. Bolden & Haki R. Madhubuti, Vol. 5, No. 1, 1999

"homeboy," "African tree," "Zoo Atlanta" & "warrior queen," *Rhapsody
In Black,* Ed. by John Riddick, Fall 1998

"America's poem, or, 81 seconds and 56 blows," *Why L. A. Happened:
Implications of the '92 Los Angeles Rebellion,* Ed. by Haki Madhubuti,
c1993

PREFACE *by Diedre L. Badejo*

In a work that is both a personal and a communal journey, Mwatabu Okantah invokes his ancestral soul as a force with which to (re) claim self and communal selves that are scattered within and beyond Africa's continental and cultural shores. Okantah's collection of poems celebrate our endurance, humanity, and myriad expressions of love, while lamenting the suffering that has marred our existence. He speaks through an ancestral soul force which guides him during a complex poetic journey that bears witness to the triumphs and torments of millions of dispersed African souls. As his mind's eye scopes our historical terrain, he pays homage to the collective pain of First Nations Peoples in the Americas. True to his cultural code of ethics, he speaks of those who first inhabited the land. He acknowledges a kinship born of mutual alienation, and anguishes with Native American peoples whose lives are decimated by disease and the death of agency. This poetic act of cultural foregrounding reconnects an historical memory that unites two earth peoples from different lands. He artistically notes that both peoples have struggled to reassemble their disparate Selves, to reconnect to their respective treasure troves. We need to reclaim our cultural inheritances, he asserts, by reconnecting through the umbilical cord of indigenous values and worldviews. Okantah's words and images capture the rich texture of these human quests.

In his article titled, "Memory Lines: Art in the Pan-African World," Nkiru Nzegwu premises that culture and memory are intertwined in such a way that visual, and by extension, verbal language embody the "politics of creation." Consequently, artistic expression can validate peoples' collective experiences, especially the experiences of African World peoples.[1] Nzegwu uses the term "Pan-Africanity" to assert an aesthetic and historical "notion of kinship and community implicit in the Diopian idea of family."[2] Okantah's introduction articulates the relationship between culture and memory. There he praises those who have shaped his poetic vision and guided him to the wellspring of his own creativity. Culturally, he locates his poetic vision at its source, known as *ase* in Yoruba parlance. That *ase* is the life force of the One Supreme Creator who energizes the human soul. Through the gift of *ase*, Okantah speaks of not only creating poetry but also becoming poetry; that is, becoming the vibratory word—speech that initiates, creates, transforms, and renews. With his *ase*, Okantah speaks as the teacher-poet that he is, reflecting those notions of kinship and community interwoven in thematic movements. A wordsmith who invokes the rhythm sounds called jazz, Okantah speaks with the voice of the old ones who intone an African-centered worldview where the orisa, the ancestors, and the unborn fuel the cycle of life itself. He calls from deep within an African perspective energizing the memories that imbibe cultural ideology and image-making. The vibratory energy that is ase invigorates the voices and worldviews that narrate a human cornucopia pregnant with all of its own contradictions. *Reconnecting Memories* reminds us that we are bound together by such collective histories wrapped in personal and communal experiences. Okantah's words become a tapestry of historical and cultural memory that demands mutual accountability and reflection.

In the collection, Okantah's concise language speaks in the polyrhythmic tones of African derived world music forms and styles of African Diasporan and African poets. He draws from a wellspring of people, events, and emotions, then he remixes them in our ancestral waters from which arises our creativity and endurance. The poet's recourse to these ancestral memories also conjures images of dancing masks through which we in the present can touch our own past and future. These masks too are shared memories from across the Atlantic from Dogon to Diop, Dunbar to Dumas to DuBois.

Okantah's sophisticated use of language, culture, and knowledge invites his readers to take a personal journey into their own deeper selves. His linguistic and intellectual tour de force emerges from a studied and lived knowledge of African descended people globally. As he remembers his personal and communal guides, his readers recall theirs. His invocation to John Coltrane's *A Love Supreme* is a healing balm, a cultural call to our collective *ase* that emanates from the One Supreme Creative Source. A*se* remembers and renews our cultural energy through the unbroken cycles of life, ancestors, living, and unborn. Okantah's personal journey and living presence marks a global kinship with people, music, and events indicative of the sixties and seventies—a time of hopefulness and challenge, inspiration, betrayal, and regeneration. Like the music that underscores his language, his collection is scored in four movements – "Reconnecting Memories," "Poet's Lament," "Black Love," and "New Afreeka." In the first movement, "black experience," he intones nightmare memories of contradictions and lies that dislodged African and Amerindian peoples in the wake of the fifteenth century European expansion into the Western hemisphere. The displacement of the First Nations of the Americas and the Caribbean Islands parallels the displacement of the African peoples who lost not only their ancestral lands but also the " sight" of those lands through the "Door of No Return." This kinetic loss of ancestral African lands is compounded by the collective loss of social, political, and economic agency, factors which continue to disproportionately affect peoples of color in the twenty-first century.

In "Poet's Lament," Okantah recalls how the imposition of European power over disenfranchised people and people of color brutalized the humanity of the oppressor as well as the oppressed. He remembers how the sense of dispossession and powerlessness creates people whose lives are mangled by self-doubt and aimlessness. Even so, he reminds us that those are the very lives through which hope radiates. In the title poem, he cleverly juxtaposes our usual gender sensibilities when he assumes the birthing role as poet who must carry words into the world. His female muse initiates the creative possibilities of such births, and becomes midwife to his poetic vision. As he later reveals in "Black Love," that female muse, is embodied as both a spiritual and human entity, who manifests in his beloved wife, Aminah. The poem also underscores the irony and pathos that accompanies his poetic vision. For example, he forces us to remember and (re) member the fragmented lives that define "Zoo Atlanta." Here his words recapture the image of black disenfranchisement that looms like a grotesque billboard over Atlanta's chocolate city where high speed black dream chasers avoid the gaze of their dispossessed kin. Who will be accountable, he wonders aloud, when some claim historical amnesia and others claim an onset of forgetfulness? He challenges us to remember the bond of ancestry and kinship between the dispossessed and those possessed by power and individualism. "Zoo Atlanta" poignantly demarcates an American racial dialectic articulated by subterranean fears that "leap out" and shatter those "wildest dreams."

Okantah calls his readers to (re) member and to remember the disaffected, crushed humanity whose souls are intertwined with ours in this historical tapestry. Exploding false media images, he writes,

> no Hollywood soap fiends to spoon feed
> the rabble daily during
> what used to be the housewife hours.
> no TV here;
> this devastation is real.
> (…)
> we see them, we wish
> not to be burdened by these

suns who somehow
never rose to shine...
(...)
our new sun
will rise from the worst
to the best in us,
and, the best
in us
has been alive
in us
all along.

From the pithy images of chitterlings and champagne to the vacant stares of the Vietnam veteran, *Reconnecting Memories* gazes at the wounds and scars of our collective paralysis and disinheritance. In gathering and reconnecting our embattled spirits, he urgently calls us again to remember a plethora of shared histories from the fifteenth to the twenty-first century. He calls us to bear witness to its latest manifestation in the memory of September 11th that sears our minds. Like Toni Morrison, he demands that we remember these experiences in order not to repeat them. And this we must do to begin healing now.

Okantah's poetic gaze also captures the self-inflicted wounds of inhumanity, greed, and racism that mark us all leaving our young to suffer a "banished peoplehood." In "he howls in the night," "homeboy," "a new sun rising," and "can we talk about race," he addresses the human cost of bigotry and oppression. Its devastation pierces the souls of a people whose muted hunger for life implodes in alcohol abuse, traumatic stress disorders, and somehow manages still to flower in the form of resistance by *living fully in this life*. And it is this resistance by *living fully in this life* that symbolizes the "spirit of the culture" found among African captives in American lands, whose *ase* resonates in music, dance, songs, and poetry of renewal. The voices of African captives defiantly claim the very freedom that their oppressors try to hoard for themselves. His words mirror such historical duplicity and hypocrisy in "red, white, and bruised," and "can we talk about race?" In speaking to the aftermath of September 11th, Okantah forces all to witness the shattered lives strewn beneath their feet, and to find amongst dead and dying their own children who hunger for redemption.

In recalling the kinship of our humanity, he evokes the spirit of "black love" when he speaks as a praise singer who first recounts his line-

age and tutelage. He conflates two central African cultural tropes, the rit-
uals of naming and verbal arts, to celebrate the central role of poetry itself
in African life. Here, women as muses, mates, and mothers with "lion
poetry roaring out of [their] eyes" envelope him in remembering the power
of ancestry in the lives of the living. In "she touched him," he writes,

> he thought about
> her eyes: dark suns, torrents
> and tales
> in and behind her reasons why.
> he thought she might be
> the woman—riddle
> to heal him from the heart-
> felt hurt he
> suffered in his time.
> she touched him in his soul.
> she was mystery
> revealing ancient secrets to him.

Okantah proposes that if we are to heal then, we must use the great Balm
of Love that all great spiritual leaders summon. In "black love," Okantah
defines love broadly as a major proscriptive cure for our multiple symp-
toms of malaise and disaffection. He narrates emotional/sensual love
between a man and a woman, the love of friendship, the love of a neo-
phyte for his or her guide, and the compassionate love that we feel when
we are touched by the purity of innocence. He sees truth and the love of
truth in the eyes of an infant or an old woman who denies hatred any
entry into her heart.

In "New Afreeka," Okantah returns to an ancestral place where the
personal and the communal intersect. "kujichagulia" for example pays
homage to the poet Langston Hughes in his work, "Black Like Me."
Okantah's poem structurally and thematically resembles this literary ances-
tor. By standing in the "Door of No Return," he (re) members and reconnects with scattered Africa; and by passing through it again, he bridges its
historical chasm and dulls its historical pain. Passing through "the Door"
also revives the kinship between Continental and Diaspora Africans, there-
by drawing upon the Diopian concept of "idea of family" (Nzegwu
2000). That notion of a cultural family resemblance appears in the poem
"breakfast at the Ibis" where kinship and the global tribal marks of a
racialized people comfort the familiar stranger in a strange land. Recalling

Nzegwu's words, "Experiences make up history and history is constituted by memories (ibid)." By reconnecting our historical, cultural, and spiritual memories, we continue to empower ourselves as we disengage from the long shadow of enslavement, colonialism, and dispossession.

Perhaps, the poet ponders during his African sojourn how distance and time have marked the experiences of Africa's dispersed children. Perhaps we do sense a different sameness, a strange unfamiliar familiarity as we locate ourselves in other lands. In "African morning," Okantah captures the cacophony of lively sounds that announce daybreak in Benin City and that are punctuated by the familiar voice of Whitney Houston on the radio. Those sounds convey the cultural synergy of a people living within time now, on the rhythms of time past, and looking toward time future. It is symphony of life found in Africa's Diaspora communities as well, and the poet recognizes the other similarities as well. For even here in Benin City, Africa's dispersed children cannot escape the changing same of poverty, harsh in its starkness yet different in its manifestation. Their faces like our faces and those of our globally impoverished children transfix us, remind us of our foibles, jolt us into calling on our *ase*. Similarly, we recognize the faces of the street people and beggars who live within diaspora cities as (dis)membered by the same greed and inhumanity, a shared experience of displacement and loss of agency.

For most African Americans especially, this is a special sensation that overwhelms us on our first landing on continental soil, and like the ocean that we cross to get there, it comes in waves. Okantah's poetic vision sees for us, as our emotions range from sentimentality to anger to regret to rejuvenation in our pleas to "Mamma Africa." Truly, this journey is the most sacred of our pilgrimages, for in it lies the opportunity to re-inter our "umbilical cord" in the soil of our ancestors, a visceral reconnection to our deeper selves. In so doing, we reunite the circle and explode the nightmare of Western captivity. At that point, Okantah intones, Mamma Africa begets us again, and rebirths us into the world with fresh eyes, minds, and spirits. Standing at this cultural crossroad, he asks, "what happens to any people who have forgotten their own name?" He again summons us to remember and (re)member the lies of history told against us. And like the Griot of the African Diaspora that he is, Okantah reminds us that the tools of our reconstruction and empowerment are found along our ancestral and cultural pathways.

To be certain, Okantah's book, *Reconnecting Memories* is a living testament to the *ase* of scattered Africa. His images and cultural tropes re-collect our scattered aspirations into a future of possibilities which rise like the *ase* of the phoenix. He closes his collection befittingly with a tribute to Queen Mother Moore. Using the style of African praise poetry, he remembers her for summoning us to reclaim our own agency and self worth. He writes,

> the road from New Iberia
> is long:
> warrior Queen Road.
> Queen Mother Yaa Asantewaa's road.
> Harriet and Sojourner's road.
> Nora Henry's African mamma's road.
> hard winding road.
> (...)
> you kept saying,
> "We Africans!
> for a long
> time.

I. Nkiru Nzegwu. (2000). "Memory Lines: Art in the Pan-African World." In *Ijele: Art e-Journal of the African World,* 1, 2.

2. Ibid.

CLAIMING MY OWN SPACE: *The Black Poet Tree*
A Personal Poetic Statement

Poetics. Poetry. Word Sounds. Energy. In the beginning was *The Word*. Utterance. Blackness. The Creator spoke the sacred Power of Word giving first light birth out of original darkness. For the poet, words exist as energy vibration. Words are living things. The word-roots of the Black poet-tree run down deeply deep into our African soul-soil. Tradition. When I looked inside my *Greater Self*, I discovered poetry. Forced into listening with my inner ear, I heard Black poem sounds calling me in a new name. When I opened my inner eye, I saw that poetry is how I see. I found oneness with the musicians and the singer-poets who have always been there to remind us that "word sounds have power," and who sing the praises of those who gave poetry its first name.

I will always remember my first encounter hearing Gwendolyn Brooks "read" her poetry. At the time, I was a 23 year old student "wannabe" poet. Miss Brooks was the featured poet at the Tenth Anniversary Celebration of Dudley Randall's Broadside Press. Her artistry mesmerized me. She leaped beyond the confining boundaries of a mere reading. I can now say she played her "axe" the same way Thelonius Monk played his piano—all herky jerky motion and syncopating, unusual rhymes and rhythms. After hearing Sonia Sanchez, Haki Madhubuti and Etheridge Knight, I literally became drunk on Black poets song-chanting their own words. I had been thrown into new space; somewhere in between ordinary speech and talking in tongues. For the first real time, I was experiencing the natural music inside Black words.

I learned to listen for word sounds. They were always in the air. I did not know it then, but, my own personal poetics were being formed; were being driven by the challenge of capturing my own inner word music on the blank, white page. During her workshop at that 1975 Broadside gathering, Brooks stressed the need for young writers to develop a healthy respect for the writing process. She directed us to study and find our own place in relation to the full range of the great Black tradition in poetry. She echoed sentiments she expressed in Broadside's *A Capsule Course in Black Poetry Writing* (Brooks, Kgositsile, Madhubuti, Randall):

> The new black ideal italicizes black identity, black solidarity, black self-possession and self-address ... the essential black ideal

vitally acknowledges African roots ... *ESSENTIAL* black litera-
ture is the distillation of black life. Black life is different from
white life. Different in nuance, different in nitty gritty. Different
from birth. Different at death.

Stephen Henderson, in the introduction to his now seminal book,
Understanding The New Black Poetry, places the poetic challenge of the Black
poetry tradition in what is essentially a clearly defined African centered
frame of reference. His essay, "The Forms of Things Unknown," had a
major impact on my approach to writing, as well as performing my poetry.
Given the present influence of Hip Hop, not to mention the use of new
technologies, I think his essay may be more important to us now than
when it first appeared in 1973. He writes, "Structurally speaking ...
whenever Black poetry is most distinctly and effectively Black, it derives its
form from two basic sources, Black speech and Black music ...."
The very title of the essay suggested a necessary focus. It articulated
what had been only a painful, nagging need that kept me awake through
long nights, and also woke me from agitated sleep each new day. Henderson provided much needed aesthetic direction. He articulated what had
been, at best, vague notions:

> By black speech I mean the speech of the majority of Black
> people in this country, and I do not exclude the speech of so-
> called educated people.... This includes the techniques and tim-
> bres of the sermon and other forms of oratory, the dozens, the
> rap, the signifying, and the oral folktale.
> By Black music I mean essentially the vast fluid body of
> Black song—spirituals, shouts, jubilees, gospel songs, field cries,
> blues, pop songs by Blacks, and, in addition, jazz ... and non-
> jazz music by Black composers who consciously or unconscious-
> ly draw upon the Black music tradition.

In this regard, I am not a jazz poet per se; although the jazz idiom has
heavily influenced the way I perform my poetry. Jazz is in my poetic concep-
tion, yet, my poetry is not limited to just one Black music form. Traditional
African sounds, reggae rhythms, spirituals, blues, gospel; that R & B glide
over a P-Funk vibration. It all rumbles in and through and beneath my poetry. At a most personal level, jazz music is important to me as a form of Black
cultural expression because it lends itself to my need to articulate thoughts
and feelings which I cannot easily or adequately express in English words.

When I first read Henderson's essay, the initial impact was revelatory. It provided me with a culturally relevant definition of poetry that made sense to my ears. I did not hear in the alien sounds of English sonnets. I did hear in the cacophony of Black life sounds that surrounded me. Put another way, Henderson's ground-breaking work allowed me to place contemporary Black poetry within the context of traditional African modes of expression: drum, dance and song—see Eugene Redmond's *Drum Voices: The Mission of Afro-American Poetry*. In African terms, the poet is both musician and storyteller. The poet is *Master of Eloquence* and *Keeper of the Sacred Lore of the Folk*. The poet is both healer and historian. The poets exist among the *Guardians of the Soul of the Nation*. From this perspective, we can consider the Black tradition in poetry here in the United States as part of an emerging, New World African tradition; a Pan-African tradition.

In the beginning, I did not call anything I wrote poetry. High school English teachers had dulled my sensibilities. Forced readings of Shakespeare and *Silas Marner* had left considerable scars. However, my first quarter college freshman English instructor gave me a new approach to the writing process by requiring each student in class to keep daily journals. To my surprise, the act of writing literally opened me up. Writing became and remains therapeutic. Subsequent professors—Hulda Smith-Graham, Wylie Smith III, Althea Romeo and Lloyd Mills—would actually see the poet in me before I was able, not to mention, willing to acknowledge it in myself.

The late Hulda Smith-Graham became my cultural midwife. Among my early mentors, she worked hardest to get me to expand my ability to see. Circumstances and her tireless insistence convinced me I had been "called to poet" during a time in my development when I needed both convincing and encouragement.

It was Hulda who had taken me to the Broadside anniversary celebration. It was Hulda who reinforced the idea of *The Griot* in my head. She was the tough minded task master who pushed me to become *more* than just a poet. It was a graduate student, Sister Odara Pat Walton, who introduced me to serious Black music. Before Odara, it was the Motown Sound and the music I grew up with in church. Integration had white washed me in rock and roll. Odara got my attention with the Crusaders' *First Crusade*. She lifted me up with Miles Davis' *Kind of Blue*. She gave me wings with the scat singing sounds of Sarah Vaughan and Betty Carter. She blew me away with John Coltrane's *A Love Supreme*. She gave me copies of Richard Wright's *Native Son* and *The Autobiography of Malcolm X* to read, and I have not been the same since. Ultimately, I cannot separate my poetry from my own personal struggle to develop and maintain a healthy, Black identity. I had no way of knowing it at the time, but the act of writing had become my primary means of self-expression and self-discovery.

Over the years, I have come to understand that I do not write poetry so much as I strive *to be* poetry. Life is poetry. We are the poetry. It is an attitude. It is a state of mind; a state of being. I tell my students that I do not believe in "writer's block." As long as there is a local bus for me to ride, or a Greyhound bus terminal to "hang out" in, I can see and experience a real poem in the act of becoming. Poetry is a way of seeing. It is a means of claiming one's own space in the world. It is a method for making sense out of this reality that would overwhelm and baffle us every day. I began writing poetry before I became a reader of it. Even now, I prefer hearing live poets. I read novels more than I read poetry. Black poetry comes out of me. It erupts. It rages. It laughs. It cries. It sings. It is.

It now occurs to me that the creative writing process, especially keeping journals, also endowed me with the aesthetic tools to explore, nurture and direct my inner voice. Writing in those early journals empowered me to satisfy this urge I did not even know existed inside of me. I learned through hard life experience that *word-sound vibrations* possess the awesome power to heal or to derange. My response to that first reading of *Native Son* forced me to discover, and then connect with my own ability to wield this power. I stumbled into a new world of unlimited Black possibility waiting for me in the reality of empty journal pages. Today, I am one of a rousing chorus of Black poet voices, what James G. Spady calls a "Muntu Kuntu Energy Poet," thanks, in part, to a college writing instructor whose name and face I can no longer recall.

Black poets are born to give life to all those unfolding stories our people need to have told. For a long time, I did not know how to describe this thing I sensed growing deep inside my being. It was unsettling. I could either give in, and become one with it, or, I could divide against myself, fight it, and experience deeper personal turmoil. Although I tried mightily, it was not in me to fight against this power. I moved toward the word sounds I heard whispering inside my inner ear. Ancestral voices. Afreekan voices. For the poets, it is not in us to fight against the power. We can only become one with it. For us, the mission is to sing a new Black oneness. My teachers helped me to understand there is no single poet who speaks for all Black people. Our strong voices together comprise an ensemble; a chorus of one collective voice. For the Black poets, our task is to give voice to those stories our people live in this world to tell.

Instinctively, I have always felt that we poets have a place and a significant role to play in Black struggle. If we are to become a psychologically and spiritually whole people once again, all of our artists must be joined in the struggle. We are the Griots. Afreekan poets. Healer poets. The roll call is long with names both known and unknown. We are the wordsmiths. We are the singers; the keepers of the story of a still scattered people who are slowly, but steadily growing back Black into one.

—Okantah, The MKE Poet
Akron, 2003

Reconnecting Memories

the black experience

whole populations have been shattered
into people who live
 jagged
edged
lives;
human fragments
in search
of discarded
memories that once held
all the pieces
together—
when everything was
not upside down:

Europe has never been a continent.
African history
is not the history of Europeans
in Africa.
African time is ancient.
African time begins
before the appearance of people
who would call themselves white.
Europe did not exist.
in the beginning
only black peoples traveled
down north
from the Mountains
of the Moon...

ii

Columbus did not discover America.
the new world
is old.
America is an alien
idea they forced into being.
it did not live
in the dream vision

of the native
people who were already
here:

the people who discovered Columbus
no longer exist.
what people aspires
to become extinct?
what must it be like to be the last
of one's tribe?
who remembers your name?
what of your memories?
no glory in Long Walks
or
    Trails
of
tears...

Columbus was lost.
he came
a stranger whose intentions
were never
good—
bringer
of our Dark Ages
our Maafa*
centuries before
the holocaust Hitler
years.

iii

so-called Red people.
"The Blacks."
Indians. Reservations. Slaves. Plantations.
"Native Americans."
descendents of ex-slaves.
disconnected peoples.
inventions.
people made figments

of a sick
imagination,
fired in the furnace
of white
supremacy—
niggers and negroes and
smiling red
sambos:

Englishmen's manifest destiny
became another name for extermination.
a bully nation
creates itself out of the destruction
of many.
Europe casts her
New World shadow
in blood,
in disease, in death—
all in the name
of some missionary
    God
no
less...

iv

strange worlds. new peoples.
how did enslaved
African mothers raise
healthy children?
old,
remembered
traditions come together
in new
ways:

Vodu.

rebel Africans conjuring in Haitian mountains.
Macandal. Boukman.

Petro.
Papa Legba
opened the gates
for the angry spirits,
for Toussaint,
Dessalines and Christophe,
for freedom.
Congolese magic
"in the Body of Dan"—
Dahomey.
Damballah. Ayida-Oueddo. Ogun
the Loas guide and
protect.

Candomble.

old Africa in Brazil.
pelourinho.
Elegbara
called the Orisa across the big water
and through the gates.
Holy Mother
Mary.
Yemanjah.
Yoruba. Ifa. Awo.
Ring Samba.
Ile Egungun—
they say the Atlantic Ocean
floor is littered
with African
bones.

North Star.

Ring Shout.
they tried to take the drums and dance away.
they forgot to kill the drummer.
we clapped our hands.
we stomped our feet.
we shuffle stepped in ritual

circle.
we two stepped
to remembered drum
rhythms.
we made a new way for the coming
of the spirit
of the Lord.

only one people sang
a new song
in a strange land.
we sang,

> Swing low, sweet chariot
> Coming for to carry me home,
> Swing low, sweet chariot
> Coming for to carry me home.

we sang,

> Everybody talkin'bout heaven
> Aint goin'there
> Heaven, heaven. . .

Holiness Sanctified Holy Roller
Wade in the Water
talkin' in tongues
Sweet Jesus rides the backs
of the weary
and wounded
opening a center beyond the massa's reach
finding a place where there was
no need to fear.

v

in this still strange,
but familiar
land,
African ancestors wander,

they are disturbed
in their eternal sleep,
they stand
knocking
at the door of our
    silence.
we
hold the key to the door.

fragments.

a people shattered
into pieces
now struggles to become whole
once again;
just inside the dark
door of our silence,
our ancestors
stand,
whispering,
trying to *reconnect*
memories—
bringing
water words
rushing
    over
us,
healing us black
into one...

            New Afreeka

*The Maafa refers to the end of Africa's Third Golden Age from the fall of the Songhai Empire and
the eventual descent into the Dark Ages of the West Africa and the European slave trading period—
1500s to 1880s, or, from the death of Askia the Great (1538) to the publication of DuBois' *The Souls of
Black Folk* (1903).

Poet's Lament
(Illustration by Al Henry)

poet's lament

she asked him about
the poetry.

how did he
tell her he was in crisis,
that his soul
labored pregnant
with words in embryo?
how to explain
the terror, the tranquility,
the black birthsong
he feared
he was being fashioned
to bear?

she asked him,
"when will you write
a new poem?"

he did not know how
to tell her
he was not ready,
felt unworthy
to carry
these wailing words
he was born into this
world to share.

she asked him about
the poetry.

slave times

... and, the sign outside the club announces:

"CHITTERLINGS
   AND CHAMPAGNE—
SUNDAY BRUNCH."

in this new
old world
slave food exists for enslaved minds.
the champagne
somehow seduces the tongue
so it tastes
something other than
captivity;
sadly, for too many,
it is still slave
times...

USA

Zoo Atlanta

the southern beauty
is always heavy
    here;
the silences
sinister:

driving through the city,
i always listen
for the leaves whispering in the trees.
an advertisement reads,
"Zoo Atlanta"(for
a brief moment i imagined
a hideous,
smiling, big lipped
black face peering back at me
from the bill board...).
i pondered the not too
hidden meanings.

on the six o'clock news
they report
a black male shot a black female
    dead
in a grocery store
parking lot.
in his mind she did not move
fast enough.
he drove his car too close.
she sprayed him
with mace.
he shot her in the chest, and
in the face.

the right people are not
talking about Wayne Williams
in this city
leadership likes to say
will be too busy to hate.

their Black American dream
is on trial here.
the dead are not missing.
they wander
the desolate streets
of our racial
    memory
by day
and by night:

they no longer
recognize us.
we have
forgotten how
to remember them:

Zoo Atlanta...

    New South

America's poem, or,
81 seconds and 56 blows

we saw them
beat him.
they beat him, and they beat him,
and they beat him,
they beat
him;
81 seconds and
56 blows.

they were tried
by a jury of their peers.
Lady Justice is not
blind.
she has been
blindfolded.
no justice.
no peace.
America's black
whitemare raging
once again in the streets:

you say
you just don't understand.
you say
we look dangerous
to you.
you pretend
you don't know why
we are so angry.
you try so hard not to remember,
you depend on us
to live and
forget:

it
began
sometime during the 15th

century.
first the Portuguese,
and then the Spanish, and then
the Dutch, and then
the French,
and then the English,
and then the
Americans
raided
in Africa.

no African holocaust memorials
in Europe
or America today,
only the Slave Relics House in Badagry,
only cells on Goree Island,
only dungeons
at Elmina
and Cape Coast castles
to remind us
the price
paid
for the second class
citizenship of an
exslave.

you say
you just don't understand.
living in ghettoes
reminds us everyday of those things
you so easily forget.
when descendents of rape
victims live
in the house of their
    fathers,
they
sleep with the enemy.
they suffer
the enemy
in themselves.

this is not the 1960s.
no Malcolm
to tell us the dream is nightmare.
even Martin said
your freedom check has been
returned,
stamped
"Insufficient Funds."
another generation
is burning
and the nation
is bankrupt
today:

you say
you just don't understand.
we live in your house.
we are strangers.
we see you in the workplace.
we are invisible.
we die in your wars.
we kill for you.
we make you laugh.
we sing, we dance, we play games
for you.
you do not see us.
you see us
only when we wreak havoc
in your streets,
framed nightly on your TV screens,
you see us only
when we leap
out of your wildest dreams.

we saw them beat him.
you say
you just don't understand.
you have eyes.
you refuse to see.
to see us

you have to look into our lives,
into that darkening
 terror
mirror reflecting
your deeply
deep felt
why:

you say
you don't understand.
you live in fear.
you have not
 listened.
you
turned
a deaf ear...

    South Central '92

he howls in the night

he lives in the neighborhood.
he howls in the night;
moon, or, no moon,
whether the moon is full
and when it is not.

what prophecy fulfilled?
who is this man?
he sings,
"I was, born, in the USA!"
in a way Springsteen never can.
his pain at depths
even stand-up comics
fail to fathom.

he has chosen slow death.
his American dream
never his to choose.
his American time lost
in white blind.
he drinks Maalox cocktails
between bottles
of cheap wine.

another good brother amongst
the walking dead.
his mind weary
inspite of the scriptures he reads;
scriptures he recalls
better than
the public believers.

another Native Son.
he journeys.
Babylon by bottle.
in our time
Bigger Thomas
is killing his Self
just being who he is.

know him.
his pain is deep.
know him.
his pain denies him sleep.
know him.
he drinks.
he howls in the night.

East Cleveland

homeboy

i remember we called
him, "Big
Daddy Elmer Cook"—
Ma Beulah's
boy.
we were in junior high school.
he was into A Love Supreme in 1966.
he was into wing'd tipped shoes,
but, he never conk'd
his head.

Elmer was into John Coltrane,
into Thelonius Monk.
he was into the "new music"
years before i would
learn it was
new.
i had been summer camp'd
into Top 40 radio "Cousin' Brucie,"
integrated into
stale "rock and roll."

i remember Big Daddy's
box front room on Oregon Street.
he didn't read comic books.
Trane music blasted
myopic Marvel Super Heroes—
like Miles Davis,
he knew the real thing.
even then, he refused to allow
the other stuff
entry into his world.
he slept in *Blues*
Minor.

the sounds in Elmer's room
saved my memory:
at Kent State i remembered Coltrane.

white blood ran in the streets
there one 70s May.
it left white
folks with a nagging after-
Nixon need
for the Average White Band—
white boys turned to black blues
in search of the soul
their own history stole
from them.

i had gone off to college.
Big Daddy went off
to Viet Nam—
neither of us came home the same.
war, and whitefolks
seared scars across the bare
flesh of our souls.
we heard it in Eric Dolphy's
Far Cry,
saw it in Monk's *Ugly Beauty*;
felt it in Bud Powell's
frantic piano
sadness;
horn solos
gave voice to feelings found in places
words dare not tread.

i remember,
we called him, "Big Daddy."
the last time i saw
    him,
he
was standing on the corner,
he had that far
away look;
his eyes set deep
in his head.

    Vaux Hall

a new sun rising

the sun rises—
another day on the urban plantation awaits.
since that first
emancipation day, slavery
has a "new wave" look
today.

each day
we see them,
descendents of the field
hands that have no
more cotton to pick.
laborers in a time
when machines
do the work of low skilled men.
loved ones turned into
statistics quoted (annually)
at professional negro conferences.
numbers ripped and read
nightly at six
and eleven.

on any given day
in the inner city quarters,
we see them,
we pass by them,
they picture-frame the reality
we wish not to face.
the script is all the way live,
not rehearsed here.
no wake up calls.
no cued studio audiences.
no Hollywood soap fiends to spoon feed
the rabble daily during
what used to be the housewife hours.
no TV here;
this devastation is real.

at the edge of the plantation,
we see them.
their days unfold
in ceremonial gathering;
the new day ritual
counting of coins always begins.
and then, the first
bottle, the one to kill the poison,
the one to blur away familiar
eyes; too familiar
eyes haunt all street
corner sadness.

as the plantation turns
these broken brothers know.
these black battered men remember.
their memories cheap wine
to be passed
from brother to slowdeath defying brother.
we remember them
as little boys, or brothers,
as fathers, as friends,
or ex-lovers.
we see them, we wish
not to be burdened by these
suns who somehow
never rose to shine...

there is no Fresh Prince
in the 'hood—
no situation comedy.
the new plantation is bleak.
what is this exslave's freedom
that gives birth
to spirit dead children
who stand staring on street corners,
who hide in alleys,
who drink a bitter wine,
who eat an even bitterer fruit,
who free-

base themselves
in search of crack-
deferred dreams?

no Hollywood South Central here.
each day, see them.
do not look passed them.
do look into their eyes.
know the quiet turbulence
raging white deep
in the private corners of most
of our lives.
who is to judge them?
we have been fooled
into withholding our strong
love...

black healing will not
be seen on television or
surround sound
motion picture screens:

see them. they are
only black men.
see in them
the depths out of which our future
must surely come:

our new sun
will rise from the worst
to the best in us,

and, the best
in us
has been alive
in us
all along.

for Omar Ali Bey (1955-1994)

can we talk about race?

i was once asked
if i only wrote poetry for black
    people?
at the time, i offered
no reply.
what could i have said?
there have already been too
many white lies.

what is there to be said
when talking to the living dead?
who can know
descendents of a self-proclaimed superior race
better than
descendents of those
forced into an inferior life-
    place?
what is to be said
to an unwilling people who
refuse to consider
a change in their ways?

one of your own poets
spoke of wastelands—
even J. Alfred Prufrock
could not have imagined this;
from lives measured out in coffee spoons
to real life lost in cyber-
    space:

i hear Babbit calling from
his middleclass grave.
his people
do not care to listen to anything
save the seductive
buzzing in their own ears.
they hear megabytes.
they hear profit margins.

they have banished true peoplehood
without a trace:

walkmans and cellular phones—
new age glitter
need not even be gold.
from play stations to the internet,
they do not know
their story has already
been foretold.
Babylon is falling, Babylon is falling
    down,
the machine culture
cannot
save anyone's
soul.

this is a poem
for those white people who say you
want to talk about race.
are you ready
to hear this land has never
been free?
are you ready
to hear we have never
known genuine
liberty?

white Americans
have been our raging
Nazis.
America has never been
what it claims
to be.

and, you ask,
"can *we* talk about race?"
but, what is really to be said when
Americans have
so poisoned the talking space?

we see you.
we see how you see yourselves.
we see your refusal
to see us.
still, you do not know how
to look into a real
black face.

can we talk about race?
the real question
is, "can you bring yourselves
to listen when black
voices speak?"
we are invisible
only because of the blinding
whiteness in so many
    eyes.
you
will never know us
until you look at yourselves
reflected in the deep
black mirror of our lives…

red, white and bruised

they call it Ground Zero,
but, others say
their chickens just came home to roost.

now, there is a rubble-
    filled
crater on the ground where
the World Trade Center towers
once stood:

the World Series
was turned into a
series of national pep rallies
where what used to be
the 7th inning stretch was reduced
to Black singers
leading baseball fans
singing God Bless America.

at Ground Zero,
there are those who wonder
if there is a God,
while their children ask
who is David
and who is Goliath
in the storyline of this struggle?

American flags are everywhere,
like sun glare—
the person driving the candy apple red
mini-van
who just cut me off
was flying one,
and i pondered those real
American attitudes
    unleashed
when
patriots get behind the steering wheel.

Americans
conveniently fail to remember
those yesterdays when
European settlers terrorized this continent
in the name of their Christian
    God—
they no longer
glamorize those savage yesterdays
when whole peoples
lived in fear of the new machine magic
of the American
way,
and ran in terror
from them.

    September 11, 2001

Black Love
(Illustration by Marcus Henry)

a poet's poem

he knew the feel.
like an old
love, he never knew
when it would come,
or, if it would come again.

the time between poems
was never the same.
hard time.
his people had forgotten
they had given poetry
its first name.

he wondered about the poetry.
amongst the poets
rumor had it
poetry had been executed,
her remains left
to the walking
    dead:

then she appeared as wordwork gathering in
his late spring storms.
(without warning)
the changing in his seasons
a mystery to him.
the poetry was there
somewhere in between normal speech
and exalted talk in tongues:

who was this woman with
lion poetry
roaring out of her eyes?
poetry always healed him.
he could look
into its window,
into his reluctant Self:

she spoke pictures to him.
she came cloud-filled.
she came stories to tell.
she came clear visions.
she came water words
rushing over
the dry well of his being—
she satisfied his need
to walk
in her early summer evening rains.

it was happening again.
he knew
this must be the way it had always been.
she came a sign.
she came symbol.
she became
poetry.
the poets were there to breathe
    new life
into
unwilling people;
to word-craft them into an old Oneness—
a new Creation Song.

the poets were there,
keepers of the sacred lore;
charged to be
guardians of eloquence;
    singers
of the
deep throated
soul of the nation.

they had been there all along...

New Afreeka

Egypt

she was a humble teller of the told story,
Ophelia Settle Egypt was her name.
Egypt, in this strange land,
this skyscraping wilderness land;
no pyramids, projects
white-promised here.

she journey'd deep south
into heartland,
into blackbelt USA,
looking for those to tell her
what it was like
to be enslaved.
she journey'd into this century
looking for those
who remembered, looking for those
who lived to tell:

and, they told her,
"I have seen the men chained together,
I have seen wagon loads of children."
told her,
"I been sold four times
and drank up once."
told her,
"We stayed there a year after the freedom
'cause we didn't have the sense
to know we was free."
told her,
"Mus'tell yo'children's children."
told her to keep our story alive,
slavery days did not destroy us,
she stood with them,
we have survived.

this new Egypt settled in the heart
of our bitter journey's
rhythm time;

from Gold Coast villages
to brick bush slums.
this black woman Egypt settled
in the womb
of our mystery's riddled rhyme,
she kept our story alive...

Ophelia Settle Egypt
(1900-1986)

see her

heavy.
you've seen her.

see her in big,
black, scarred woman eyes.
always, you see it
in the eyes.

see her
early, on workdays,
waiting patiently, too
patiently, on the
bus, her bus,
the Short Hills bus.

see her,
dark, African
looking woman;
feet flat flaunting years
stood upon; stiff starched
uniform white covering
knees gnarled
kneeling, scrubbing, scouring;
bones bent keeping
someone else's house clean.

see her,
each new day,
talk to her,
listen:

> Ma Beulah say, "Son, ya know,
> now ah bin workin'
> in whitefolks' kitchens
> mo'sa my life,
> an'ah was sayin'ta my missus
> jus'the otha'day,

"Ah say to her,
yall shouldn't oughta hate us,
yall should love us,
Lawd knows we could kill ya
if we choosed.

"We cooks yo'food,
we suckles yo'chirren,
we tends yo'houses,
yall should jus'love us
'cause it jus'aint right to hate,
Jesus weren't like that,
it jus'aint right to hate.

"An'ya know son,
all she could do was
look at me
'cause she know it
jus'weren't nuthin' left
to say."

see her,
tired, trudging
homeward.

see her.
know her in your eyes...

Ma Beulah Cook

to a black woman

she did not know
she could touch him in his wordlove.
she was only being herself.
there was no warning,
no way for her
to have known...

as if out of a dream,
she came to him
in a line of poetry.
he chanted her name
to fill the void
only his silences could bear.

she did not know.

outside the dream,
he searched for her inside
the quiet mine of his poetry,
reached out to her across
the wide canyon of his fears,
across the deep
space of running years
emptying into time's winding stream.

she did not know
how she had touched him,
touched into him,
into that secret sacred space,
that night private place
where poets go
before the words become
a poem.

no one could tell her...

it surprised him
to meet her in the poetry,

walking along
the shores of his dream
filled days.
she could not know
he would see her,
still, standing there.
she could not know
the poetry waved his high tide
tension out to a calm sea.

what was there to tell her?

inside his dream,
she could not
know he would delight
in her garden.
how could she know
he would find
her waiting
for him there?

who could have told her?

she could not know,
inside the poemlove he would find
her waiting for him there...

Aminah

she called out to him

listening to the silences
   echo
inside
his night,
he waited for
the soft sound of her
voice whispering his name.

she came to him
out of her own deep longing.
she saw blackness
in his eyes
in ways he could not,
in ways he could never
see it in himself.

she called out to him
from her
   distance.
she
knew his voice.
it comforted her.
she called out.
she softly called
his name.

he spoke red earth words to her.
he sounded depths
from their sacred soul
   soil.
their shared words
became bridge spanning
their wounded
and separate worlds:

she called out to him...

she touched him

she touched him in his soul.
it was not in him
to fight against the feeling.
he was humbled
inside the reality of his pain.
his longing told him
he needed
to rediscover the tenderness
he had forgotten
he held inside.

to know love was not
new to him.
how many times had
she visited him in his imagination?
the memories haunted him,
sharpened the edges
of his searing silences;
the silences echoed
deep into
the caverns of his regret.

she made him
think about life alive
living all around him.
he thought about
her eyes: dark suns, torrents
and tales
in and behind her reasons why.
he thought she might be
the woman-riddle
to heal him from the heart-
felt hurt he
suffered in his time.

she touched him in his soul.
she was mystery
revealing ancient secrets to him.

he knew her.
she was the moon
moving through phases reflecting
soft light as he
searched in the far corners
of his own wonder-
filled night.

she touched him in his soul.
she was songbird
singing,
perched high up in his poetree
scat singing harbinger
melodies.
silver and gold
music.
he heard her.
her music moved him
to fly free...

how many times

how many times
will i walk
with you
under whispering trees
in our season
in my mind?

how many times
will i look
in your eyes
in my mind
searching out my Self
in your eyes
in my mind?
how many times?

how many times
in my mind
will i give you
this poem
these soothing sounds
quieting this tension
i feel in my mind?
how many times?

how many times
will i meet you
in my imagination?
how many times
will i attempt
to give of my Self
to you
in a poem-song
that begins in my mind?

how many times?

song for Aminah

you asked if i could
write you a poem,
not knowing how i have wanted
to sing you a love
song:

love is the light
that glows between us,
so i am singing this love song
for all those times
when (even for me) the simple words
i love you
were not enough:

like the moon, like the sun,
we are one
in the same sky—
the connection was there
from the first moment
i looked
into your eyes.

you asked if i could
write you a poem.
for us,
making love became literal—
when i met you
i met my soul mate.
inside your brown woman
black love
i found safe space.

you asked
if i could write
you a poem.
i could not tell you
that poem
has been growing inside of me
into this love song...

New Afreeka
(Illustration by Al Henry and Murphy Ajayi)

kujichagulia

in the beginning
we did not
   call
our
selves black,
we were black
in being
deep
as the original night
that gave birth
to first day:

thought. word. utterance.
blackness.

ii

our great men and
our great women
walk
amongst us.
know them when you
see them.
do not be in
fear of their black
 light,
it is there
to heal us after
our long journey through
whitemare days
back through
what is no longer
a "Door of No Return"
into night...

for Ed & Shirley Crosby

breakfast at the Ibis

each morning
she slips in a side door.
only i notice her.
circumstances make me
a willing accomplice.

hungry people roam streets
everywhere
in this world.
in picture post card
London, they
haunt train stations,
Bobbies herd them up from underground:

in hotel restaurant
she stands
still,
statue-like, mindful
not to disturb
the thick European air;
India beauty,
battered,
too far from home
to be hungry in strange lands.

English, American, French, German
tourists breakfast
at the Ibis.
they have European eyes.
they do not see her.
they stare.
they pretend they do not see me
sitting there watching
them.

through white shadows
only i notice
she has dance-dared-

dared-to-dance
about the buffet now.
our eyes meet.
tray in hand
she makes her way to my table.
invisible.
we both eat.

London

African morning

the cock i never see
crows each
new day to announce the sun.
a goat bays,
his bell ringing
just below the compound wall.
morning birds
sing solitary music
to clear Benin City air.

children on the way
to school
sounds
rent the stillness of the Sun's rise.
a woman sings as she draws
water.
Whitney Houston
songs startle
on the clock radio.

African city sounds begin...

Nigeria

market day

the light flashes red.
traffic stops.
the intersection transforms into market.

they come. they converge
on waiting cars.
people selling all manner of things:
leather goods,
toilet paper, razor blades,
chew sticks, groundnuts,
newspapers, magazines,
handkerchiefs,
baby clothes...

they come.
beggars on twisted limbs
with probing eyes.
blind men guided by grim faced
sad eyed children.
children.
refugee women, wandering, babies
carried in their arms, babies
tied to their backs, babies
held up before open
car windows.
they search each car for soft eyes
to look into...

the light flashes green.
traffic resumes,
the people retreat,
they wait—
the people market each day in Port Harcourt.

   Nigeria

poem for Africa

oh Africa,
so many would seduce you,
so many would make you
the harlot of all the lands.

oh Africa,
which way will you choose?
money lust will destroy you.
vampires already
taste your black blood.
corporate vultures circle.
they smell green death in your air.

Africa, my Africa,
what good is progress
when ancient traditions give way
to white hot madness,
when virtue runs like oil
between the legs of your daughters
turned street walkers
in port city nights?

Africa, my Africa,
hear our cries.
hear the children of those taken turned
American ghetto dwellers.
we know the pale menacing glare.
we know the hardheaded burden
we see you so
determined to bear.

Africa, my Africa,
Mamma Africa,
even in America
a new Griot tradition
sings freedom wake up
songs for you—
neither centuries

nor distance,
not even our own demon
ignorance
can deny you
in the center of our days.

Africa, my Africa,
Mamma Africa,
we come
home to you,
to embrace you,
your power,
to sink our roots back
into your profound brown
navel of the earth
love.

our face
is your face
is the same face:

we are one.

New Afreeka

African tree

Nigeria's giant silk cottonwood,
massive,
mystifying, majestic,
standing the tallest tree in the forest.

mighty tree, how many rains,
how many dry seasons
have you wind-song weathered?
how many times
have your leaves whispered
the stories of black ages?

talk to me old African tree,
tell me our story
from unknown pages.
talk to me,
master of the forest tree,
pointed skyward,
grayish green white against the horizon.

teach me to stand
Nigerian tree.
your kidnapped
now lost
children are in need
of tall trees
to grow
masters of our hostile forest.

i stand in your shade
charmer tree,
rid me of this bitterness,
bind these wounds,
heal these scars lashed across
the bare flesh
of my imagination.

restore me magical tree,
resurrect Africa's
dispersed children once more
upon that stage
of our history
only you in your tree-
wisdom can know.

grant me harmony
old African tree, protect me
inside the Ogbunike cave*
black warmth
of your long shadows.

i stand before you ancestral tree,
envelop me
in the darkness of your
Niger area
love...

Nigeria

*Ogbunike Cave is near Onitsha and the Niger River in the midwestern region of Nigeria.
It is a location where Africans hid from slave raiding parties during the Maafa period.

Rite of Passage

what was once real
now lives inside the imagination—
the middle passage is
now
a journey
we suffer in our minds.

an elder brother
looked at me and said,

"Write me a poem
'bout why
young people today
don't relate
when we tell them we used
to have to wear
cardboard
in the bottom of our shoes."

i looked at him
in wonder.
i wondered.

how to teach a generation
to stand their
 ground
when
they are unsure
and have no real sense
of the ground
upon which they stand?

i wondered,

what does it mean
to be
a black poet during hard
times when so

few black people
feel the need to gather
   together
to hear
black stories whispering
in the leaves
rustling softly high
up in our own
 poet
tree?

i wonder...

ii

he continues to sit there,
black lion
dread
locked into
ancient serenity facing
east,
facing each
new day sun's rise.
why Greeks
renamed him Sphinx
("The Terror")
is all but forgotten today inside their lies—
that black
ancients once named him,
Heru of the Horizon
now calls out
for a new Sun
to rise.

what was once
   hidden
in
darkness
is now becoming known
in a new light:
names.

the Greeks renamed *Kemet,*
"Aey Gypt Ptah."
for them
it was "The Land of the Temple
of Ptah."
it became Egypt.
our story has been
lost
   inside
alien names ever since.
we have
become
a still wandering
people
in desperate search
of our proper
name.
what happens to any people
who have forgotten
their own
name?

iii

what kind of seeds
did our African
ancestors
   sow
for
us to have reaped
these days
in confusion and pain?

there are no
new places for us to run,
we are left
to face finding
   real
truth
somewhere deep inside this uncharted

New Age
Afreekan terrain.

up from Booker T's,
"Cast your buckets where
you are . . ."
to DuBois' *Souls of Black Folk.*
up from Garvey's
"Forward Ever, Backwards Never," to Malcolm's
raised from the dead level
street corner Mother wit.
up from King's
3rd generation black preacher's
earth rhythm eloquence:

our new scribes
have placed original
Her-em-akhet
once again on
the eastern horizon of our consciousness—
the *Eye of Heru*
is reopened.
our singers and poets dare to proclaim
to all our generations:

in this now time,

know that you stand
on the shoulders
of giants—
know
the sure
ground upon which we stand.

    imani

warrior queen

My brother, better mind how you walk on de cross,
    De young lambs must find de way,
For your foot might slip, and yo' soul git lost,
    De young lambs must find de way.

—Traditional

"Speak, Garvey, Speak!"

the hall
is filled with people.
the atmosphere is electric.
i can see it now,
as if it were just yesterday,
as if i were there.
i see you,
that pistol packed away in your purse,
another concealed
in your bosom.
everyone had come prepared.
freedom was there
to grasp with our own hands
on this night.
even the police knew
to leave well enough alone.

"Africa for the Africans,
at home and
abroad!"

Black Star Liner.
Garvey
said, "Up you mighty race,
accomplish
what you will..."
you were there.
you stood. no fear.
you dared.

in Muscle Shoals. in New Orleans.
in Los Angeles. in Chicago. in New York.
in London. at the UN.
you cared. you organized.
UNIA. Republican. Communist.
Ethiopian Women. Mt. Addis Ababa.
Republic of New Africa.
you said, "... fifteen cents
an hour,
it was just like slavery
time."
you told us, "I ain't askin' for no bill,
I demand reparations!"

the road from New Iberia
is long.
Warrior Queen road.
Queen Mother Yaa Asantewa's road.
Harriet and Sojourner's road.
Nora Henry's African mamma's road.
hard winding road.
Queen Mother didn't have to change your
name because you were already a
Moor road.
you were out there saying,
"We Africans!"
for a long
time.

Queen Mother Audley Moore
(1898-1997)